T4-AEC-054

# In the Right Season

# In the Right Season

Diane Sher Lutovich

Sixteen Rivers Press · San Francisco

Copyright © 2005 Natasha Terk
All rights reserved
Printed in the United States of America

Grateful acknowledgment is made to the following publications, in which the following poems previously appeared: *Cloud View Poets:* "Love, Sex, and Illness"; *Marin Poetry Center Anthology, Volume VII, 2004:* "Album," "Just Blocks from Here," and "When Assumptions Are Not Enough."


Special thanks to David Madway for his support of this publication.

Cover photo by Jeff Braverman

Typesetting and cover design by Laurence Brauer, Wordsworth, San Geronimo, California

Published by Sixteen Rivers Press
P.O. Box 640663
San Francisco, CA 94164-0663
www.sixteenrivers.com

ISBN 0-9767642-0-2
EAN 978-0-9767642-0-5

*For Natasha*

# *Foreword*

"A very *not* PC cancer," she termed it, the virulent pancreatic cancer that, as Diane Sher Lutovich learned in the fall of 2002, had laid claim to her life. Then she launched full-scale into the business of living as long and as fully as she could manage—with joy, wit, and courage—precisely the way she had always lived. In a New Year's 2003 e-mail to her friends, she wrote:

> At this end of 2002, a year that brought me news of a most difficult cancer, I find myself going over all I have to be fortunate for. Sometimes I forget entirely what lies beneath and call myself one of the world's luckier people. And, of course, I am. I have enough money to pay for any drugs yet developed. I am surrounded by the love of family and friends. I have a loving companion who comes with me to my treatment each week as an act of solidarity, and still likes to have sex and get stoned. In the backyard the camellias shout out their joy at making it to another season, and the wisteria buds reveal hints of a luxurious spring not too many months off.
>
> In my drawer, airline tickets to both Mexico and Paris, and within the hour, my grandson will be here to spend New Year's Eve (along with the champagne guzzlers).

For those of us privileged to share that last year and a half with her, Diane was truly an inspiration. She traveled, she worked, she took classes, she made new friends, she reveled in the pleasure of longtime relationships. And through all of it, she continued writing poems. Most poet-friends who heard her work at informal readings and workshops were struck by its power and ranked these poems among the finest she'd ever written—no small accomplishment, considering the fact that her prize-winning collection, *What I Stole*, had come out in the spring of 2003.

This book, *In the Right Season,* contains almost all the poems Diane wrote during those last months of her life. Within weeks after her death on June 2, 2004, a group of us who loved Diane—and her poems—started working almost spontaneously toward making certain that this final legacy of hers would come to life in print. The members of Sixteen Rivers Press, the Bay Area collective she helped found, immediately agreed to publish the book, and lent their expertise toward helping shepherd it along. Her critique group—Barbara Swift Brauer, Kathy Evans, Doreen Stock, and myself, who had listened to each of the poems through multiple drafts—acted as the editorial staff. Her companion, David Madway, and her daughter, Natasha Lutovich Terk, lent support at every turn, along with wise, intuitive advice at moments when we reached for the choices Diane herself might have made.

For all of us, I believe, and most certainly for me, this project has provided an opportunity to engage in a profound healing process. That art can grace its gifted toilers with immortality remains one of life's most reliable miracles. For here, among these pages, we find Diane again—laughing, complaining, considering, affirming—and always very much alive.

—Jackie Kudler

# Contents

## *A Gathering In*

- **13**    A Gathering In
- **14**    It's All Real Estate
- **15**    One Day, Two Dragonflies
- **16**    Two Views of Spring
- **18**    Gray Is Not a Color
- **19**    Winter Skies
- **21**    Just Blocks from Here
- **22**    Power of the Ephemeral
- **23**    Love, Sex, and Illness
- **24**    In the Right Season

## *It's About Time*

- **27**    It's About Time
- **28**    First You Want to Talk and Then You're Not Sure
- **29**    Nights in the Gardens of Brooklyn
- **30**    When Assumptions Are Not Enough
- **31**    Album
- **34**    Sharing the Dawn
- **35**    Remains
- **37**    For a Short Time It's Here and Then It's Gone
- **39**    The Dead Are Too Cold

*Shot into Space*

| | |
|---|---|
| 43 | Shot into Space |
| 45 | Floating Bodies |
| 46 | All of Us Must Have Turned Away When It Happened |
| 47 | A Human Torch |
| 48 | A Very Special E-mail |
| 50 | Try to Praise the World Filled with Sorrow |
| 51 | What Sinks Doesn't Always Rise |
| 52 | It's All Just Temporary |
| 53 | Traveling as a Tourist |
| 54 | In the Wholeness of the Universe |
| 56 | How Long Is It Until We Get There? |

# A Gathering In

## *A Gathering In*

Shedding her solitary
flesh slowly, she
boxes comfort
of nesting habits
of books and bowls
knowing which window leaks sun,
how moon silvers her world,
direction of knobs, hiding place
of keys, where glasses go
when they disappear,

geese clamoring, knocking
sounds like breathing
packed into boxes
shifted to a new
spot on the map of her mind.

Out of some
primitive instinct—
think hatching turtles
scurrying to the sea,
cats licking afterbirth—
she moves toward
a place of *we*, a word,
despite so little breath,
still sticks to her tongue
like salt.

## *It's All Real Estate*

After so many years
of locking our own doors

coming together to trade only
bodies, stories, glasses of Merlot

then withdrawing to clocks we calibrate
and blankets to hedge against cold

until last month when Big Red and His One Big Truck
moved what I love best—the engraving

of the famous artist's wife with her sharp nose,
photos of parents shrouded in youthful hair,

silver bowls and photo albums
showing my daughter's increasing size,

all of it into a house you called
*mine*, into corners you forgot.

We dropped our costumes, wigs, releasing
something sweet and savory, started spiraling up,

silent touch replacing loud sounds, quick brushes
leaving skin fragrant, gentled.

It is, of course, all a real estate of pronouns—
*his, hers, ours*—but sometimes in consolidating,

in closing in, one finds an opening out.

## *One Day, Two Dragonflies*

Two dragonflies, oblivious to their beauty,
copulate on a July afternoon.
Their sleek gold-flecked bodies,
the blue and green of beach glass,

lift just so, one on top of the other.
It's that simple: in suspension,
weaving their next generation
into a sun just breaking through the fog.

I take their rocking and vibrating as a gift,
memory of times I didn't need a bed or bedroom—
any place for aching instincts would do—
kitchen, mountaintop, hospital room.

I still see the two of us, swinging gently,
our colors flashing in the sun as we lay
one on top of the other, suspended by hope,
flashing the iridescence of instinct.

## *Two Views of Spring*

Gray cubes of wind
clang into cans and cars
where lilting should be
the rhythm and curves the skin's
response, but branches have been set loose
snapping, whipping
back into themselves.
Green leaves look sallow, shallow,
like color peeled back
by relentless bursts of air
shifting from one trunk to another.
Teenagers march on by:
large-footed, foreboding, five abreast,
smashing into each other,
kicking whatever presents itself
to their feet.

Just one tulip from the
Luxembourg Gardens
would change the angle,
one mauve-colored tulip, each cupped
petal curved like a child's ear
to take in sounds
of flesh sparkling
in a sun-warmed afternoon
where children
set their sailboats loose
on the pond to make
broad circles like a watered
finger around a wineglass, around and around

and nothing breaks or kicks—
air so soft it curls
around the tongue
and sneaks into each
slippery place hiding fallow
under the tongue
where the taste of Paris sets thickly,
long after Paris has
receded to the ocean's other side.

## *Gray Is Not a Color*

Gray skies are not hopeful. What passes for sky on this typical Bay Area summer day feels like an ether mask pressed close. It's gray with life sucked out, color of my mother's face just after she died. It could be my cancer making me despise absence of sun, beg for some light, hues of hope. Or maybe not.

So I focus on chasing
down color much closer
to the ground. Find poppies
crusted in gold, blue jacket
of the toddler running by,
purple delphinium,
pink-throated roses,
faded red flags promising men
working, a burgundy car,
yellow daisies,
orange nasturtiums.

When I look even closer, the greens explode into
a hundred shades—chartreuse of the newly hatched and
near brown of the old leaves, ready to break free.

From my window, the ancient oak and younger eucalyptus
almost cover the sky with their green, but where they leave gaps,
a dour and defeated sky peeks through.

Newspaper promises more of the same.
I would almost die for sun—that yellow globe
passing as god's eye, a color to warm the soul.

## *Winter Skies*

1.
At the Pacific on this cleanest,
brightest of winter days, with the sun striding
close to the horizon, its reflection
splits the water into billions of shards,
each reflection forcing a new reflection.
I would splay myself on the waves, daring
the sun to send a spike of light right through
me, pinning me to the Pacific, forced endlessly to roll
in and out as if that's all there is, just rolling in
and out.

2.
Sky so pale and wispy,
clanging of garbage trucks sucking up
neighbors' drained bottles and screaming
orange peels. I get an update on her granddaughter,
born three months early. Now it's her heart,
always her breathing, always tethered to monitors.
For three months. I report on my tumor—stable,
that's good. Around the first corner, baby stores full
of cornflowered dresses and wings, tricycles with
and without pedals; around the next corner
we start the incline as if
everything will be better once
we reach the top where it levels
out. We round the track
as many times as we can,

start our descent. Smells of fried chicken rise
from Safeway, green papayas sliced
in the window of the Burmese restaurant,
plastic fish swimming around the artificial pond
in the sushi bar. Cars stop to let us cross.
Past Albertson's, Zachary's Pizza, sky dims to a wash.
Do I feel grimmer, more helpless when
it's ready to rain? The sun, after a very long run, has
turned its back. It's a day in which I want to be nursing,
see milk flow from my nipples into a waiting mouth.

## *Just Blocks from Here*

five or six of them stand
on the green concrete lawn,
cigarette smoke wafting from their clenched fingers,
as they push their ashes, butts into the large Folger's coffee can,

their faces sweet and beatific—
whatever medications they're taking
erase all tension, terror from their faces,
children's faces, really, on old men's bodies.

Sometimes one walks by heading for Albertson's
to buy more cigarettes, speaking loudly
to whatever devil haunts his imagination.

At night, the dim gray light of a television leaks through the shades.
Later, house dark, all the men asleep in their beds, meds
swallowed, easy dreams.

If they looked in a mirror, they'd see
a certain good fortune,
their faces unchanged for the last twenty years,
even when they're shouting at the sky.

Their faces look absolved of living,
of crimes they never committed.

## *Power of the Ephemeral*

Shadows from the oak branches
scuff across the deck, always
in motion like a parade or army.
Lacking color and substance,
they engage the fence and tremble
like fingers exploring a body.
They could be a tongue of flame,
exchanging heat for cool
afternoon breeze, but they
hold the eye, even more than
the oak trees themselves only
yards away—because, I think,
they are untrustworthy,
unsubstantial. Something
to deceive and hold you
while the real action goes on
somewhere else.

## *Love, Sex, and Illness*

How sensuously he removes the old bandages
while I sprawl on the bed, mostly naked,
as if we were preparing to absorb each other.
The same fingers that gently
explored, exposed my body now detach
the line drawing bile from deep inside.

His hands so determined
I barely dare exhale,
can see the intense gaze, the same way he used to look
at my breast, the curve of my elbow.

And my gratitude swells to the top,
the way it does when I come—
each time as if heaven were full of promises
and we were full of faith.

Later, he puts on the fresh rubber gloves,
tenderly closes the wound, remembers
to say I love you—we keep discovering new forms of intimacy.
Two people who have traversed so much of life
together and apart—coming to trust
hands and body, as if that's all we have.

## *In the Right Season*

In these rains, camellias, large as soup plates,
cling to the branches that birthed them.
Bursting with juice, they turn
their faces in every direction—no
pattern or posture to their hanging.
When a breeze tosses them,
I can almost hear them murmur through the walls.
The lower branches, ones I can reach,
are bare and seem very brave; remaining ones
are safe from me and my clippers. A squirrel
dashes clumsily across the garage roof, dislodging
one of the sweetest, which nuzzles the dirt.
Soon they'll be gone; plum blossoms
already skate along the fence, wisteria, a few feet away,
will start purpling up by next month.
Two raccoons copulate in another part of the yard,
making more raccoons to dig up the grass.

In each new sign of life, I hear him saying,
"How will I live without you?"

# It's About Time

## *It's About Time*

Today I want to invite the dead in,
show them to a well-padded chair,
offer a cup of chamomile tea, finally
ready to listen to them talk
about pain, narrowing of the spirit.

When they were dying,
each of my joints was a well-lubed machine part,
stomach ready for chocolate malts, stuffed peppers,
martinis, fried calamari, coffee as thick as sand.

Today, we could discuss levels of pain.
Now I inhabit the body of the stricken,
maybe temporarily,
maybe not.

"Here, I'll turn up the heat,
lower the shade against the too-bright sun,
bring a down pillow for your neck."
Instead of turning away from their decay
I'd kiss each one of their pale,
sinking cheeks and tell them,
"I know."

## *First You Want to Talk and Then You're Not Sure*

The year-old wants language with the fervor many of us want to abandon all words, all means to talk about feelings. Babbling incessantly—soft sounds like munching crackers or sucking a nipple; when need overwhelms, a shriek that consumes his twenty pounds into an explosion of high C. The first time I saw white cut-outs falling from clouds, I screamed "feathers!" My mother taught me the word *snow*. Cradling the phone in his right fist, the toddler cries wet tears when it rings into his hand. Yesterday I received a note from an old friend responding to news of my cancer: "I remember a kiss in an elevator. Can't forget it. Don't want to forget."

## *Nights in the Gardens of Brooklyn*

Like an old lover's name. Unheard or unseen for more than four decades, jumps from the paper and each syllable feels like a kiss. "Nights in the Gardens of Brooklyn": my song, my truth, my Torah and midrash, spoke to me of how I lived or should live—I remember something about painful love, about not getting, only wanting. I tucked a paragraph or two in my purse, like spare change. I thought it could save my life in a pinch. Some days I'd take out those words, like a moon, and weep; something about happiest or least happy. Suicide, walking into the newly discovered Pacific, looked good. Barely twenty, I was going to weep another thirty years before I discovered there were things even better than crying. When the author died, he was much younger than I am. Maybe he would have changed. But I'm not sure about any of it. I could hunt down the story, find those words that I fondled until only smudge remained.

## *When Assumptions Are Not Enough*

Perhaps you knew you'd been only
a mistake, a slip of the condom during a night
of too-careless love-making, eggs so fertile
they would have trespassed through clover, hay, mucous,
cell walls to catch that spilled sperm—
letting the body know briefly swelling
of breasts, chunks of nipple.

I assume you knew you were never
to feel grass between your toes,
milk drip into your budding lips.
You wouldn't know the horror
of sliding through that bloody tunnel
into the arms of people waiting to hold you.
You'd never have a name.

So you never had a chance. Nor did I, I'm afraid.
We stayed on, your putative mother and father,
but only because of you, long after you were extracted,
buried or burned, my womb stuffed with gauze
to soak up your bloody beginnings.

Forty years later, when I see a man who would be about your age
crossing the street, I remember careless sex
with terrible consequences. That man, any man
could have been you—fingers starting
to twist, hair, which never had a chance,
starting to thin. The stoop of someone who was never
a child, ghost of my youth. Those days when the future
was like a movie I had to save up for.

## *Album*

1.
When I picture my dying brother
strapped to his hospital bed,
I see a mummy in the Cairo Museum
wrapped in flesh-colored bandages,
only his eyes, mouth uncovered.

His eyes stare at the wall, I, straight at him,
the way we never looked at each other
in real life. But this last time, I look closely.
For a second, his eyes focus on me, enlarge with astonishment,
or fear. His mouth forms a terrifying circle.
As if he is five and seeing for the first time a sister he didn't want.
Someone should have taken our picture.

2.
In earlier photos, I wear a white bonnet and gloves.
He wears his blazer and white pants. We stand
in front of the beat-up house on Sixth Avenue. The one we
moved to as the Depression thickened. For the rental
over the garage, Mrs. Hill paid twenty-five dollars a month
and stayed until the cancer finished her
some time after VJ Day.

I shipped these pictures of our childhood today.
Oakland to Minneapolis, they keep circling
the country, a stop in Denver before
and after as if we can't find rest.

We don't stop on anyone's shelf—one niece wants
to show them to a cousin, another sends them to old
friends, as if they're made of something lighter than
photo paper—spirit. Each time a picture
slips its socket, another takes its place, and
the little girl is now stuck over
the name of her father's German shepherd.

3.
Our mother, keeper of memories, must have lost interest,
or the Brownie broke, or maybe
she was too depressed seeing herself getting older,
growing from girl to thick-middled woman.
Maybe she knew it was already over.

It was before my brother left for college,
before her husband died. But one day
she put down the camera and said "That's it."

4.
My brother used to let me ride
on the back of his bike holding tight
to his chest, played quarterback, starred
in *The Mikado* and wanted
desperately to keep living—even after
everything was gone.

I couldn't comfort him.
He was unable to form my name.
I don't know if he saw me.
I was part of a different life.
We never said good-bye, or see you around.
But I told him, in case he could hear, that we did the best we could.
Someone should have taken our picture.

That's what pictures capture best, that it's
over. One of those could be called the last picture.

## *Sharing the Dawn*

This cool gray morning, throwing on my gray sweats,
I remember mornings on Sixth Avenue,
sub-zero weather permeating every wall in the house
except the pink and green Marolite bathroom where the heater
blows soft summer air while my father
showers, shaves (first mixing his lather of white clouds,
stropping his razor, leveling his face, always careful
to leave his mustache unmarred), dresses,
and I, the only other one awake,
am invited to sit on the covered toilet,
warm my toes and fingers.
He turns away while naked
so I catch only the smallest glimpse
of his penis. I thrill at the sight of this appendage
between his legs, think about
elephants I'd seen at the zoo—exotic,
wild, something that seems out of place in
the house on Sixth Avenue.

Dressed then, in his suit, white shirt and striped tie,
ready to cook oatmeal for my breakfast.
Before leaving the room, we turn off the heater. By that time
the rest of the house has warmed up.

## *Remains*

We buried my brother a little deeper,
        climbing Red Mountain, blue sky crashing

into red sandstone as remaining family recall

        how much of him we carry deep in our bones—
        irreverent humor, caution, desire to control—

as if he had splintered into shards,
        each shard landing deep inside those who shared

the same gene pool, back to Izzy and Florence,
to Sam and Nellie, Bellah and Jake,
        and farther to some shtetl in eastern Europe,

a million miles from the red rock buttes
of southern Utah. At night, stars danced in close,

        full moon cast a circle around our complicity,
air clarifying the spaces

        we inhabit—even day and night.

And someday they'll gather at another mountain,

        tell stories, recognize the connection

as deep as the roots of the oak tree outside my window.

Native Americans made baskets of memories
                for elders to take to the other side.

But living and dead cross back and forth;

                lines between this side and the other
are not solid, crumble like sandstone.

# *For a Short Time It's Here and Then It's Gone*

So much of what's disappeared came from the center: jade beads, each rolled into a heartbeat, chunks of turquoise hammered from rock, strung

between shells from a sea on another planet

Uncle Harry's fob watch, his newly crafted American initials HWS traced like wisteria on its golden cover

The Omega watch that plunged me into marriage in 1965, its mechanism slowed through disuse, while a certain knot of affection kept time years after the decree

> *Disappeared*

Earrings my father bought for my mother months before his cancer, the family legacy, carried him beyond sight of ears, earrings, bills

Chip-size diamond baguettes left from the wedding ring he bought for her on the eve of the big crash (borrowed the money, they say)

> *Gone for good*

Amber earrings, several pair, bought by different lovers in some unnatural attempt to preserve, beautify the past after it's over

And don't forget the carnelian necklace from Jerusalem, lapis earrings modeled from an ancient Greek artifact, my high-school class ring, National Honor Society "H"

*Erased*

Somehow, the whole family shrunk, tumbled
into the jewelry box—receipts dating to the treaty of Versailles,
a memento for every human atrocity

For each piece, a face—father, mother, me as a young girl festooned
in second-rate jewels for a future of lascivious riches, long before
skin and hair disintegrated into its own kind of memorabilia, torn
out from the center of the earth

*To which it will all return—lost, stolen, dying and dead*

## *The Dead Are Too Cold*

At the cemetery, a cold wind whips off Lake Superior chilling the path between car and tombstone. After all these years there they are, side by side, the way I used to see them through the keyhole of their bedroom door, spying, hoping they'd notice, invite me to join them in the wide four-poster. They pretended I wasn't there.

This time, among the birches and the summer green of Minnesota July, cold wind whipping off Lake Superior, they don't know, can't know I'm standing nearby, that I had come to touch the place they last had form. I have nothing for them but bad news. Not even stones to put on their stone. I want to see myself as pure in the cold wind, someone who would come thousands of miles to see slabs of marble with the names of the parents who had rolled together and caught fire—for me— they caught fire and I come empty handed.

I run to the car for warmth, unable to mouth a few platitudes for the dead. Running away, I know I won't be back. I want to be burned by a fire I never knew in life and scattered in some place where the sun will be hot and loved ones will come leisurely to visit. I ask for nothing more.

# Shot into Space

## *Shot into Space*

Sun shadows make angles
while we draw from each other
power to put words on paper.

Across the veiled light, the bay's
rolling waters connect us
to the world of commerce where
tall white buildings,
like temples at Karnak, preside over
cars, money, and homeless looking
to shelter their bags and cans,

into the first level of sky where
clouds inflate and deflate,
leaving us in shadow and light
in a nation that learned to mouth
*preemptive strike,* and babies lisp
*shoulder-to-air missile,*

back down to the family where
the toddler points
to the plane buzzing overhead
with or without an armed marshal,
practices *no* and *please*
and the power of *your hat is pretty,*
pushing his new birthday front-end-loader
across the field waiting for lunch or his blanket
or the warmth he's come to expect;

around the world, snipers in Baghdad, orphans in Kenya,
pre-pubescent sex girls in Bangkok,
all the way to astronauts circling the planet, seeing
splashes of light sometimes
interpreted as hope.
No blood, no killing, quiet, they say,
breathless, they add, the way it should be, with all color
and anger stripped to a glimmering bone
up high enough to scrape molecules of dead parents
whirling in space as if they're going to the store for more milk,

back to the couch where I sit fully formed,
pen in hand, looking
as hard as I can to bring it all to my breast:
the living and dead, homeless and homed,
protected and vulnerable.

## *Floating Bodies*

Do you remember the first time you discovered your body could unanchor? Could float free, propelled only by pleasure and fear? The way your father drove to the top of First Avenue—fast—and while the gray pre-war Lincoln-Mercury crested, your stomach flew to the top of the car and your body forgot who and what it was. In a town prairie-flat, he found the one best hill for surfing. Those eye-blinks lasted forever. *Again*, you begged, *again*. Only silence and screaming. Only fear of living and fear of dying. Each time, it was the way the stomach moved up through the throat, through the top of the part in your hair, and you were attached and unattached at the same time. Much later came the same unanchoring, when Sam put his fingers on your ripe nipples, and much later the same feelings of dying.

Now as doctors can say only *who knows*, remember again how bodies float free, the sticky too-sweet surge in the back of the throat (too much chocolate ice cream, for instance), that and the wonder of the ancient redwood, ancient oak outside the window. As if it isn't all just a series of lift-offs, floating, returning to base, wherever, however that might be. And still the echoes of *again, do it again*.

## *All of Us Must Have Turned Away When It Happened*

*After W. S. Merwin*

The night the sperm swam smack into the egg and formed
a new life.

When the bad cells vanquished the good ones, started
their slow ramble onto destruction.

When the mother announced she was dying, and the
brother retreated into his final coma.

When the fertilized egg emerged into a fetus, and
clouds lifted the top off Mt. Tam.

When the oceans gave up their last fish, and
the little girl jumping rope passed 250 jumps.

When the leavened bread rose up to the ceiling,
and the cook left for a new job in a munitions factory.

When the Cracker Jacks turned on the prize and smashed it,
and the last independent bookstore closed its doors.

When the tank was empty, pens ran out of ink,
and all the blank paper fueled fires.

When the sun called together its glowing embers
and decided to rise one more day.

## *A Human Torch*

Instead of smelling the December evening wind,
we were buried by the stench of his burning skin and hair.

Even this morning, putting my fingers to my nose,
I smelled the rancid, randy smell of flesh burning,

the smell of my mother's kitchen when she held a chicken
over a gas flame to remove its pinfeathers.

Hardly enough soap to erase the smell, painted on with such
  a thick brush.
An exploding log thrown down to stoke the fire, a scream
  too feral

to have been human. In a flash, scents of evergreen, bayberry,
sounds of Mozart, Dylan fled the room.

It was hours after the fire that the images of the Holocaust
  started hovering,
stories of whole villages of Jews locked in barns set on fire,
  their flesh

condensed into wisps of smoke spiraling upward, caught by
  winds and clouds
moving them farther from home than they had ever dared to
  wander when alive.

Twenty-four hours later, I still gag on the odor. Olfactory
  senses meant to track
food, warn of danger, carry their own memory.

It could have been any of us floating aloft;
only the smell of our burning reminds.

## *A Very Special E-mail*

To: Daren Pack, Summer Fun, and Angelina Mercer

I appreciate your offer of something to remove unwanted hair. I have no unwanted hair. Because of my chemotherapy, I am missing much of the hair I actually want. When you're into adding hair back, look me up.

To: Holly Parks, Raleigh Freije, and Tasha Warren

I don't want to see what you have to offer, no matter how hot and wet it might be. Now if you could offer to show me something that is cold and dry, I'd be interested.

To: Geraldo Zavala, Andy Masters, and Rodrick Quinon

I don't know why you think I need to improve my sexual performance. Have you been talking to someone about me? Is there just something you could suggest by e-mail?

To Brigitte Schaffer, Benita Quigg and Homer Beck:

I think it is great that you can offer me something better than Viagra. But I'm a Viagra virgin. And oh Lord, I just can't take any more than I'm getting. Try again in about six months.

To Marlene Gilliam, Gloria Esme, and Phil Summers:

Thanks for your offer to reduce my mortgage. My house goes on the market tomorrow. It's a long story, which you'd probably rather not hear. Suffice it to say, no home, no mortgage.

Thanks, anyhow.

## *Try to Praise the World Filled with Sorrow*

*After Adam Zagajewski*

The pale rose blooming
      from the plant you thought dead.
      Watching each person you love
      sit down at one table,
      those chosen tongues
      tripping over language, weeping with
      efforts to form sounds.

Remember the wind whipping tears
      from your eyes as you ski,
      hips turning just so, speed almost unbearable.

Remember how to provide comfort,
      wrap your arms around
      the grieving and frightened.

Praise the world so full of
      sorrow and hydrangeas
      the color of Zinfandel, and the first light
      blossoming through the shades.

## *What Sinks Doesn't Always Rise*

Stuck in the bottom of sleep,
each time her body
tries for release
to rise
to float
to watch the sun start—
limpet, dumpling—heart
so heavy, surface
closed.

Sub-basement, third level,
no air, no leaves, no lips.
Reaching for release,
she almost reaches the surface.

Panic, antic, romantic,
she dreams she makes it back.

## It's All Just Temporary

For sixty-five years I took for granted
the sweet peel of tangerines,
stopped wind, wisteria over the garage,
mornings with French roast
and steaming milk, a run alongside blue herons,
fast-footed egrets, and at night,
pillows cradling heads and mattresses caressing bodies.

And then one day I was reminded how temporary it was.
I was a guest—well fed, even admired and respected. But
permanence was not inevitable—
a myth perpetrated by Miss Stone in kindergarten.
She promised we would go on to first grade,
letters would become words, our bodies would grow.


So when the surgeon said *we can't, you must, we will*,
he drew a heavy drape between what I knew and what I know.
Stars still shine at night.
Waves still spit angles of foam into
the receding shore. And I am a guest on this planet,
staying only as long as the days promise
a resting point each night
and a creeping color each morning

when black recedes into a cavern where it, too, is a guest.

## *Traveling as a Tourist*

Suliman Bay, shockingly calm, curving,
separated from the Caribbean's endlessness
by a reef throwing up capes of whipped foam;
swimming, snorkeling for sight of a ray or two, sipping margaritas;
burglars second-storying the house at night,
stealing back loose cash, driver's licenses, cell phones,
staring into our sleeping faces sleeping on their land,
rich Yankees hiring them to cook and clean
feeling good for saying *buenas dias*
as if they give a damn for our fractured Spanish, and the water
so clear you could count coral beds from two stories up,
bottle glass where greens and blues coagulate, disintegrate,
trips to Muyil, Coba, Tulum at dusk where Mayans worshipped
time and dates with gods who asked heavy jungle dues
a thousand years ago amid blood, palms, and mahogany.

And at night, a fiesta where toddlers, spit and polished,
wander with ices while a dehorned bull
rushes a toreador holding a bath mat,
and we all hang on to each other, because
we are in Mexico and the air is too sweet, the sounds
from Iraq and Washington on another channel
drowned out by mariachis circling the fiesta, making the fiesta,
and when the trumpeter lets loose, I know I want to live forever,
swimming in Suliman Bay, sipping ices, grinning at children,
thumping my own breast for having come this far.

## *In the Wholeness of the Universe*

Orbit of life, the way it goes out,
comes back and continues
to circle, picking up stray neurons
and discarded particles,
the way even separated
friends combine their yin and yang into
a perfect sphere.

Everything is round. Start with
hands on the belly, the round belly,
plump fist.

Then everything circling
back to the beginning.
Roundness of the sun flying up in the first morning,
snowballs and snow creatures.
Fear forming huge circles on steamed
windows, ghosts' mouths, and
first scoop of vanilla ice cream.
Roundness of bodies twisting in sex,
buttocks forming orbs in each hand,
sounds of cherries bursting their flesh,
juice dripping from peaches,
belly during pregnancy,
infant curled into a ball;
roundness of its first laugh and its
first recognition.

The moon has no place to go but back
to the almost-circle in which we all sit, forcing words
spiraling through the body, coming to rest
on a slip of paper,
where they live on past the fullness, roundness
of time.

## *How Long Is It Until We Get There?*

I will travel to the end. I will go by scooter so I can use one foot to help. No engines, nothing of this or last century. Maybe I'll switch to horseback if I get tired or have mountains to climb or my leg gets too sore. I will not be in a hurry. I'll stop to drink water from streams and pick the fattest blackberries, fix salads of miner's lettuce. At night, I'll stop where the breeze is soft and count stars, no longer bothered with the names of constellations. I'll use morning light to start a fire, heat water, check my bearings. Bearings, like directions, irrelevant because no one knows where the end is. But I'll start out each day, stopping to look up at the tops of redwoods or down to the rocky bottoms of mountain streams. I'll use my skin like a circumscribed conduit and check/determine temperature, directions of hairs, permeability of confusion. It will be a new kind of trip, not like flying to Paris or sailing to Phuket. Those destinations have signs announcing their/your place in the universe. When you're heading for the end, you'll find arrival, at first more ambiguous and then suddenly you'll know—you'll see it in the faces of those you love, you'll feel it in the circular breeze bouncing off your breasts, you'll smile, even laugh. You'll have arrived. It won't matter the year, or time of day, or how much light remains. You'll feel rested and sated. You'll feel it was all a journey.

## *Diane Sher Lutovich*

April 30, 1937–June 2, 2004

Diane Sher Lutovich grew up in Hibbing, Minnesota, and moved to the San Francisco Bay Area shortly after graduation from the University of Minnesota in 1959. There she remained for the rest of her life, working, writing, and raising her daughter, Natasha.

What began as a career in public-school teaching developed into Advanced Communication Designs, the training and consulting company she co-founded in Marin County, and where, for twenty-five years, she conducted business writing workshops for corporations and government agencies.

She started writing poetry in 1976 and went on to publish her work in numerous literary reviews and anthologies. She engaged, also, in a number of creative prose projects. After her mother's death in 1994, in one such instance, she spent many years researching and writing *Nobody's Child: How Older Women Say Good-bye to Their Mothers,* which was published by Baywood Press in 2002.

Diane's first full collection of poems, *What I Stole* (Sixteen Rivers Press, 2003), received a 2004 American Book Award from the Before Columbus Foundation, and was a finalist for a 2004 Independent Publisher Award.

Diane's last days were spent at home, surrounded by close friends and in the company of her beloved daughter, Natasha, and her life companion, David Madway.

The text for *In the Right Season* is set in ITC Esprit, designed by Jovica Veljovic. The display font on the cover and section titles is Lithos, an Adobe Originals typeface designed by Carol Twombly in 1989.

The book was printed by McNaughton & Gunn, Inc., Saline, Michigan.

Sixteen Rivers Press is a shared-work, nonprofit poetry collective dedicated to providing an alternative publishing avenue for San Francisco Bay Area poets. Founded in 1999 by seven writers, the press is named for the sixteen rivers that flow into San Francisco Bay.

Also from Sixteen Rivers Press:

*difficult news*, by Valerie Berry

*Translations from the Human Language*, by Terry Ehret

*Snake at the Wrist*, by Margaret Kaufman

*After Cocteau*, by Carolyn Miller

*What I Stole*, by Diane Sher Lutovich

*Sacred Precinct*, by Jacqueline Kudler

*No Easy Light*, by Susan Sibbet

*Falling World*, by Lynn Lyman Trombetta

*Swimmer Climbing onto Shore*, by Gerald Fleming

*Mapmakers of Absences,* by Maria M. Benet

San Joaquin * Fresno * Chowchilla * Merced * Tuolomne
Stanlislaus * Calaveras * Bear * Mokelumne * Cosumnes
American * Yuba * Feather * Sacramento * Napa * Petaluma

1815

NORMANDALE COMMUNITY COLLEGE
LIBRARY
9700 FRANCE AVENUE SOUTH
BLOOMINGTON, MN 55431-4399